The New Oz

The Wizard Revisited

Richard Marvel

Valkyrie Publishing House

St. Petersburg, Florida

THE NEW OZ: The Wizard Revisited
Copyright © 1992 by Richard Marvel

published by
Valkyrie Publishing House
in cooperation with the
Foundation for Human Potentials, Inc.

First Edition

International Standard Book No.
0-934616-45-0

Library of Congress Catalog Card No.
91-066695

1992
Printed in the United States of America

*Dedicated to the human race upon planet
Earth, without whose help this book could not
have been written.*

Acknowledgments:

... to Marjorie M. Schuck, the one person that I would like to single out for being the most helpful in actually having my ideas published. Without you, Marjorie, this book would still be just a dream.

... to the Foundation for Human Potentials, Inc., for their interest and encouragement.

... to all the musicians who performed and produced the songs mentioned herein.

TABLE OF CONTENTS

AUTHOR'S PREFACE

Much has been written on the subject of ESP, Extra Sensory Perception, but what does it mean? To the majority of mankind, ESP remains a bit of a mystery... a subject that most people have difficulty relating to, a talent claimed by a few but elusive to the many. What if there were a simple way to awaken your own ESP ability?

This book is such a "tool". In it, the author will show you one function of ESP by example... like learning how to swim, or ride a bicycle, or play a piano. Once you have grasped how to do it for yourself, all future progress then becomes self-directed.

Life is an adventure and a mystery, an experience to be enjoyed to the fullest. In his own personal lifetime, the author found himself to be a member of a generation that observed monumental changes occurring in the way that life is lived day to day. Through his own life and experiences, he hopes that others can relate to the changes that have happened within America (and to planet Earth) during the 20th century.

In the time that it takes you to read through this material, you will discover something that is a part of your world but is not immediately apparent... something part mental and part physical that does not become "visible" until you first develop the pattern by which to see it.

If you were born before mid-century, then you have witnessed most of the changes

brought by technology through your own eyes
and ears. If you were born after mid- century,
this book can serve as a sort of review. During
the remainder of the 20th century, our world
is a mixture of those who can remember a time
before television, and those who see
technology as having "always" been a part of
their life.

Humanity is now experiencing a basic
change. This new awareness has already
happened to some, and will happen to many
during the decade of the 1990s. It is a psychic
awareness. The author hopes that you will
enjoy your experiences in this new world of
ESP and psychic reality... it is a lot like your
old world, but different.

Richard Marvel

St. Petersburg, Florida
November, 1991

The Quest
(A Theme for the '90s)

We search for our ancient homeland
Wide-awake inside the dream
We come through the fifth dimension
To hear, to touch, to see
We bring the myth and the magic
And the memory of our song
The time has come to bring you home
The trip will not take very long

We appear at the dawn of a new Age
We usher in the change
For every human now alive
The world will be re-arranged
Don't wait too long to join us here
As we play out among the stars
And bring the Golden Age to Earth
From a time and place called New Oz

1: The Journey

*"In the shadows of a Golden Age
a generation waits for dawn."*

JOURNEY, 1983
Only the Young

All must walk their own paths as they travel through life, and sometimes strange and wondrous things are encountered along the way. Life seems to be a multitude of mysteries afloat on a sea of human emotion. As individuals, we sometimes search for the meanings to life's mysteries. We attain varying degrees of success based upon the interpretation of our own personal lives, and the empathy that we share with others.

The story of a New Oz has to do with the similarities found in life... how certain things remind you of other things... how one thing is like another. Originally conceived after the author experienced what would be called a "vision quest", he brings his story to the world so that others can also take part in the discovery.

After nearly being struck by lightning, he set out on a journey to get some advice from the leader of a psychic research group. He encountered a terrible storm... with thunder, lightning, and multiple tornados... then was lifted up into a dimension *above* time and space. After that, he met with the leader, who informed him that he already had the potential to be what he wanted to be. The leader then suggested that he go back home and re-evaluate what he already had. Sound familiar?

To the author, it was like combining the story of Dorothy in the *Wizard of Oz* with the lightning bolt transformation of the comic book character "Captain Marvel".

The author's birthday was about a year after the debut of the MGM movie *The Wizard of Oz* and "birth" (first issue) of the comic book character "Captain Marvel". The similarities between both of these works of fiction and the journey that he had just experienced were both apparent and unexplainable. How could such a thing be possible... how could something that was supposed to be a fantasy actually happen in "real life"?

Never in his wildest dreams had he ever believed that each and every person also exists in a parallel dimension, another mode of consciousness existing *above* the material plane we call planet Earth. Now he could verify this through personal experience. As an expanded awareness dawned within the author's life, he noticed relationships and interactions in his day to day living that he had paid little attention to before. Things seemed to fit together in mysterious and unexplainable ways. A story began to emerge combining the present moment, the future, and the distant past into a single concept.

After the vision quest experience, the author realized that he had suddenly gained psychic abilities he did not have prior to his journey. There appears to be a psychic doorway between dimensions, and this door can only be opened from the inside. In some mysterious manner, his journey through life had led him to this door. He was then able to open the door and move into another dimension of reality. This turn of events was totally unplanned and unexpected.

> *"All in all,*
> *The journey takes you all the way*
> *As apart from any reality*
> *That you've ever seen or known."*
>
> YES, 1972
> *Close to the Edge*

2: Home

"Starlight movement,
Reasons release forward
Tallest rainbow..."

YES, 1973
Dance of the Dawn

After returning to his home in Florida, he saw his surroundings in a different light. In addition to his newfound psychic ability, he was able to re-enter the upper dimension by an act of willpower. Similarities arose that he had never noticed before... the city in which he lived reminded him of other times, places, and events. Relationships formed between the world of today and the world of history. Music came alive.

The 20th century generated four major events in America and the world: (1) *The Wizard Of Oz* book by L. Frank Baum, and the MGM movie classic of the same name; (2) the growth of technology; (3) the re-emergence of the Mayan civilization out of the jungles of the Yucatan; and (4) the birth of "Rock Music".

By combining these four events, then looking for examples and likenesses of them in his hometown, the story of a New Oz was first conceived. Since that time, 1973, the story has grown... supported by "new" events that entered the world after that particular point in time. The remainder of this book is the telling of the New Oz story, written to demonstrate how the upper dimension is reflected in our world of today.

> *"Right here, right now,*
> *Watching the world wake up*
> *from history."*
>
> JESUS JONES, 1990
> *Right Here, Right Now*

3: REDISCOVERY

"I'm learning to fly,
but I ain't got wings."

>Tom Petty, 1991
>*Learning to Fly*

During the last 50 years, the world we live in has been dramatically changed by technology. Even greater changes are now surfacing within the human race, but on a psychic level. The future is here now, awaiting your discovery. By using mental patterns that are older than this solar system you can learn how to access another dimension of reality. To do this, you must first discard the childish notion that "everything began here on Earth"... we are *not* the only life-form in the universe.

You won't find the subject of a New Oz being taught in any school. It is an ongoing event that is happening *now*... if you know what to look for and where to look. There is a movement, a change being brought to planet Earth, a re-awakening of a mental ability "lost" thousands of years ago. You can be a part of it... perhaps you already are a part of it. Everything in our physical world originated in the mind... first an idea; then a reality. In the decade of the 1990s, the human mind is presently experiencing a metamorphosis. We are all being changed. Once you see what is going on around you, you can join those of us who are actively bringing this change. It's your move.

Is this story fact or fiction? You must decide for yourself. The difference between fact and fiction is that fact is "lived out" in the world; fiction is confined to a person's imagination. At first, it seems like a dream, but then you find that New Oz is *real*. The proof is discovered when you take this concept out into the world and see for yourself what is here.

Most Americans were told stories about Santa Claus, the Garden of Eden, and George Washington chopping down the cherry tree while they were still children. During the present 20th century, American children learned a new story... a story about the Wizard of Oz. Each of these stories conveyed information to the child in terms that the child could easily comprehend. As the child grew older and matured, some of these stories were discarded as "fantasy"; not found in the real world.

Looking back at world history from our present moment, only the names of people, places, and events made manifest in our world are viewed as being real. The debate still rages between evolution and creation theory. A third alternative has emerged during the 20th century... planetary reincarnation. This "new ordering of the ages" provides an alternate view of the life and history of planet Earth by synthesizing evolution and creation in a unified story that describes "a New Oz"... a new planetary dimension (home) within this solar system.

Names and events in the story of New Oz are verifiable; they are easily found; they all fit together and unfold through historical time in a sort of "slow motion" interaction... lived out in our real world. When you see how all of the parts of New Oz are linked together, you have personally taken a giant leap towards Extra Sensory Perception (ESP).

Perhaps you missed it the first time around. If so, you can review your own life and experiences. Look over your books, records, and tapes... the story is there. As you begin to see the reality of a New Oz in your own life and how it applies directly to you, how it pertains to other people in your life (and to the whole world in general), you have started upon a journey of rediscovery. You know what to do... "follow the yellow brick road".

> *"Slow motion riders*
> *Fly the colors of the day..."*
>
> **CHICAGO, 1974**
> *Saturday in the Park*

4: Oz

"We were timeless dreamers
of another day...
In a dawning Age
we had so much to say."

BOSTON, 1986
Hollyann

The average American has spent the early years of life in some type of formal schooling: elementary, high school, college, and perhaps even higher. However, learning about the world is a life-long experience... it doesn't stop when you leave school, it is just presented to you differently.

Some of the things that you learn are given to you in ways that you don't even realize that you are being taught something. The message is very subtle. Some of the greatest teachers in the world today are not recognized as teachers; they are called *entertainers*. You can find them in the arts (in movies, television, and books), and especially in the field of music. It is in these areas that you will find the concepts of a New Oz... a new planetary dimension. Through the lyrics of many entertainers, a single theme emerges

The name "Oz" should be well known to virtually every American. First shown on network television in 1956, the MGM movie *The Wizard of Oz* has been broadcast throughout the United States of America every year since 1959. It is acclaimed as the most popular and most widely seen movie in the world. First published as a book in 1900, The Wizard of Oz has been translated and printed in more than twenty different languages, truly an "American dream" shared with the world. However, the story does not end there.

What is not so readily known in today's modern technological world is that the name Oz is quite ancient in origin... the population of Atlantis called their land Oz. In the Bible, that land is referred to as Uz. Today we call our land the "US". When author L. Frank Baum used the name Oz, the label on his filing cabinet drawer, it was a serendipitous synchronicity relating to both mythology and history. Let us look more closely at the story of The Wizard of Oz.

Contained within this American classic is a key that will unlock a secret history, a hidden knowledge. Although L. Frank Baum wrote this story as a children's fantasy, it can also be interpreted on a metaphysical level. Looking back over the 20th century, aspects of The Wizard of Oz can be seen as a parallel to the emergence of technology in our material world as it presently exists at the turn of the 21st century. One example is the visual effect used in the MGM movie... the transition from black and white to color. The birth of television also evolved in this pattern. Let us reflect on this story.

The Wonderful Wizard of Oz, the first of a series of Oz books by Lyman Frank Baum (1856-1919), was published in 1900. The success of his musical stage adaption "The Wizard" (which played from 1902 through 1911) caused Baum to shorten the original book title to *The Wizard of Oz*, which he did in 1903. In 1904, Baum published a sequel, *The Marvelous Land of Oz*. In all, Baum authored the first 15 of what are now an Oz collection of 46 books.

In 1914, L. Frank Baum formed the Oz Film Manufacturing Company, producing four black and white, silent films.

After Baum's death in 1919, the rights to the Oz material were assumed by his son, Colonel Frank Joslyn Baum. Colonel Baum began negotiating with the MGM studios in 1924. A movie contract between the two was finally signed ten years later in 1934. MGM hesitated to produce what they considered to be a children's story until 1937... when the studio saw the popularity of the Walt Disney movie *Snow White*.

The production of the movie began in 1937. It would take two years to complete, use 9,237 actors and actresses, occupy 30 soundstages at MGM, use 68 different sets, and cost over three million (1938) dollars. The movie debuted in August of 1939, and quickly became a world-wide sensation. In 1949, MGM reissued the movie.

By investigating the symbolic content found within the movie version of *The Wizard of Oz*, another way is found to interpret the development of the progress of mankind on planet Earth. The relation of the upper dreamlike dimension of Oz to the lower dimension of Kansas is a modern re-telling of the story of Atlantis brought up to date.

In an ancient time, before time began upon this planet, seven Elohim came to this solar system to observe the Earth at it's creation. The Elohim are the mythological elders of the human race... they are the guardians of the memory of other planetary civilizations.

Some people view the Elohim as either "gods" or "angels"; some consider them to be universal forces at work within our galaxy; others have never heard of the Elohim. However, their story is very interesting when we all realize what is actually in our world of today. The Elohim were said to come from another dimension that was "above" time and space... a reality found on the other side of dreams. After the birth of our planet and solar system, six of the Elohim returned to the upper dimensions of super-conscious reality... one of the Elohim remained behind to guide the human race. This Elohim occupies the symbolic aspects of the Moon, our nearest heavenly neighbor, and is said to guide humanity through the subconscious interaction of dream and emotion. The Elohim symbolize and manifest the "sacred seven" on Earth, and are symbolized in our visible universe by the Pleiades star group.

The Pleiades are called "the seven stars", though only six main stars are visible. At the vernal equinox of spring, this star formation is positioned directly overhead, over the point of the Great Pyramid of Cheops. From this famous and ancient structure, the beginning of each new Earth year (cycle) is aligned with the Pleiades. In addition to the Pleiades, that particular location in the heavens (28 degrees of the sign Taurus) is also home to many other sun systems and/or galaxies positioned behind the seven stars.

A mental projection of the Elohim named Uranus (the first king of Atlantis) generated inter-dimensional forces, then lowered their vibrations, causing these forces to descend (cross) into Earth's three dimensions of length, width, and depth, thereby experiencing "time", the fourth dimension of this solar system. These mental forces merged with physical earth life-forms to produce a race of humans, a combination of mind (upper dimension) and Earth matter (physical body). Thousands of years later, this story would again be symbolically written and re-told in biblical terms... the story of life being brought to planet Earth.

The entities of the prototype race born

upon this planet were inter-dimensional beings able to move in and out of a unified and collective planetary consciousness, a non-material dimension that is "above" our three-dimension Earth reality, just like in L. Frank Baum's story *The Wizard of Oz*. On Earth, these entities were to introduce technology into this solar system, thereby producing a Golden Age of advanced living. Instead of this expected progress came the cataclysm... the "submergence" of Atlantis, when the human race became cut-off from its own memories of the past.

Atlantis is not about THIS planet; it is about a planet that we all once lived upon (like the story of Krypton). Because of the physical characteristics of this particular solar system (the fifth planet was destroyed), the human race soon became individualized. Surviving man identified himself as a race of separate individuals, wherein each individual ego attempted to prevail over all. Group unity disappeared... Humpty Dumpty fell. We forgot. Many thousands of years would pass before mankind could once again rebuild the "lost civilization of Atlantis" upon this planet. In the flow of time, a new Atlantis would re-appear in the world. At the turn of the 21st century, mankind has put Humpty Dumpty back together again. Technology has now re-emerged in our world, and psychic abilities are returning to the human race. Atlantis has been reborn on this planet with a new name. This time, we call ourselves Americans. Many of us presently live in a new nation called the United States of America (the US). *Oz is US*. In the recollection of the past, our returning memories are recognized once more in the 20th century story of Oz. We remember a "time" before this planet physically existed.

In our newfound homeland upon planet Earth, returning memories are seen within the story of Oz. Characters in the colorful land of Oz are dualistic, they are based upon the symbolic representation of similar characters in the black-and-white, three- dimensional world of Kansas... each person in Kansas has their symbolic counterpart in Oz. The location of Oz was "somewhere over the rainbow", another dimension found on the other side of dreams, just like the dimension that is home to the Elohim.

In addition, other aspects of Oz help us to interpret our present world of today. The three characters that accompany Dorothy along the yellow brick road can also be seen to symbolize the three factors of modern civilized man in the 20th century: (1) the Cowardly Lion as man's animal nature; (2) the Straw Man as man's social self; and (3) the Tin Man as man's technological self. All are on a journey leading them toward a meeting with the wonderful wizard in the Emerald City.

At the turn of the 21st century, our entire planet is entering a New Age, the Age of Aquarius. Humanity is now moving away from the restrictive "black-and-white" of the Piscean Age (we forget) and into the colorful light of the dawn of Aquarius (we remember). Memories older than the Earth itself are resurfacing within our minds. As a New Oz was being revealed within America during the decade of the 1970s, it's birth was symbolized by a rainbow.

The rainbow has, in virtually all times, places, and civilizations, symbolized some kind of "doorway" or "bridge" between different realities; different worlds. As the New Age emerges, a New Oz appears within our mind and thoughts like a rainbow.

Rainbows form at an angle of 41 degrees to the Sun... violet and indigo blue form at 40 degrees; blue, green, and yellow at 41 degrees; and orange, red, and infra-red at 42 degrees. The movie *The Wizard of Oz* was popular in movie theaters worldwide during the years 1939-42... the same time period in which the realization of mankind's technological rainbow became visible in our present-day world of material reality.

The Age of Aquarius can also be symbolized by a rainbow, as "something carried in water". In addition, the symbolic representation of the sign of Aquarius found within our solar system is the planet Uranus, the ruler of the sign of Aquarius, and the legendary first king of Atlantis. Some of the specific influences attributed to Aquarius and

Uranus are: waves and wave propagation; universal vibration; electricity; electronic technology. Aquarius symbolizes all things transmitted and received, such as radio and television waves.

Viewing the 20th century as a whole is quite enlightening. From the years 1900 through AD 2000, we can see the emergence (or re-emergence) of technology on this planet. Technology now gives us a kind of "artificial eternity" where we all can manipulate time and space at will, planet-wide. We have taken upper-dimensional, eternal concepts and applied them to living in the flow of time in our 3-dimensional plane. We can now play recordings that are magnetic, optic, or digit based; captured on cassette tapes, CDs, and VCRs. We now have instant access to global events as they happen through television. We externalize abilities of our conscious mind, projecting our intelligence into "programs" used to run computers... mind-augmentation tools that extend our mental abilities and capabilities.

We no longer have to attend "live" artistic performances in person; we can now watch and listen to movies, radio, and television series re-runs featuring actors and actresses that have since died, and enjoy the music of artists and groups that have disbanded. We have digitally recorded sounds and images that will endure for the rest of mankind's existence on Earth. All of the "time" has been removed. Upon Earth we have built a global technology that is operated by individuals... in our home (or in our car) each person can now use technology to individually transcend "time" and "space" on this planet.

Along with technology, the entire human race is regaining it's original state... we are all becoming telepathic. As we move into the Age of Aquarius, a new inter-dimensional doorway has opened to humanity, allowing our conscious mind into the upper dimension (Oz). Millions of us can now access this thought transfer dimension.

Many of us have achieved *dream control* reality. Projecting into our level of everyday living, we have now superimposed concepts of Oz. Suddenly the entire human race is regaining a conscious ability to experience a reality on the other side of dreams... awake. We have regained the access to a 5th dimension "above" the limits of this planet and solar system. Up, up, and away...

> *"I opened my heart*
> *to the whole universe*
> *and I found it was loving.."*
>> **THE BYRDS, 1966**
>> *5D (Fifth Dimension)*

5: Music

"Dawn of love sent within us colors of awakening among the many want to follow... only tunes of a different Age."

YES, 1973
Dance of the Dawn

In the last chapter, you discovered the key concept linking Atlantis with the name Oz... they are one and the same. In today's world there are many instances of the re-emergence of the abilities attributed to the Atlantis civilization. This is no secret. Within the population of planet Earth today are many that are starting to "remember".

All over the world, there are many people who have experienced a *conscious* awareness of existing in a dimension transcending space and time as we know it. Books have been written about this phenomenon... the "out of body" or "near death" experience. At present count, there are 8 million Americans and as many as 50 million people worldwide who have admitted to this experience... existing in a 5th dimension that is non-material and totally telepathic in content. If you are one of those who have had such an experience, you are not alone. Far from it, for there are many like you upon the Earth at this time.

If the truth of the matter were known ahead of time, it might have caused a panic among the populations of Earth if the story were misunderstood without the proper preparation. The translocation adjustment has been spread out over thousands of Earth-years. During the 20th century, an extensive educational program was carried out to prepare humanity for the restoration of ancient memories. To discover this for yourself, the best and most obvious example that you should investigate (and the area in which the most obvious examples are to be found) is the category of popular music. Contained within the songs of the 20th century, and most noticeably the decade of the 1970s, you can see a new *planetary* dimension awakening.

As our long-lost abilities begin to re-surface within the human race, the reality of a New Oz becomes visible. You don't have to wait for a future time for this to happen; all you have to do is look back a few years. It is (and always has been) in the music... just put all of the pieces of the puzzle together. The New Oz has been here for quite some time now, just waiting for the proper moment to be recognized by mankind. Now is the time.

The maturation of technology upon planet Earth during the last half of the 20th century brought its own music, an artform in itself, electronic music played through electronic instruments. From its birth in the early 1950s, this new form of American music was designed to educate the younger generations on a subconscious level. It is a music from and for a different Age; it is a new form of communication with its own message superimposed. Using music as a "vehicle", the memory of who we really are has been returned to planet Earth. The story can now be told and understood.

During its infancy, this form of pop music was looked at in "black-and-white" terms... you either loved it or hated it. Disk jockey Allen Freed, broadcasting nightly from radio station WINS in New York City, coined a name that stuck. He called it "Rock and Roll" music. Today "Rock" music has evolved and expanded, becoming the most popular type of music in its time... "pop music".

Pop (Rock) music was born in the early 1950s, the forerunner of computers and the transistor, a "rock sandwich". Take two crystalized rocks; glue another kind of crystalized rock between the other two; add electricity, and presto... a transistor.

Popular music electronically recorded and reproduced; music played upon electronic instruments. The story echoes throughout the history of humanity... *We step upon the rock.* An expedition to our solar system from another star or galaxy that landed upon the Earth could say, "We step upon the Rock (planet). We come from the other side of the sea (space)." The *Mayflower* crossed the Atlantic ocean, and the Pilgrims said, "We step upon the Rock (Plymouth). We come from the other side of the sea (Atlantic)." In this New Age, reawakening Atlanteans can say, "We step upon the Rock (music). We come from the other side of the sea (dimension)." It has all been captured in the lyrics of popular songs.

The entire category of pop music is not all good or bad, it is more like a rainbow... there are many different hues and shades of color present. Pop music is not all black or all white, though there are instances of both contained within it. Instead of making a blanket judgement, let's try to discover the message that has been superimposed on and transmitted through electronic music during the decade of the 1970s.

Found throughout the history of pop music is the theme of a New Oz... going through the changes in between Ages, the outgoing Piscean and the incoming Aquarian. For reasons that will become crystal clear in the next few chapters, the New Oz influence was more or less centered around 1976, America's Bicentennial Year. It was during the decade of the 1970s that Oz-related bands appeared upon the music scene... KANSAS, RAINBOW, TOTO, and HEART.

Other groups and individual artists tied in to the story by name or subject matter... the lyrical content of their song. Examples of this are easy to find. For instance, the first hit recorded by the group the 5TH DIMENSION was "Up, up, and away... (in my beautiful balloon)"... how the Wizard originally traveled to Oz. Their second hit record was titled "Aquarius/Let the Sunshine In". During the 1960s, the BYRDS recorded an album entitled *The Fifth Dimension*. For all to see, the New Age and the re-emergence of Atlantis was set to music, a collective effort that shines through the songs and the artwork of the latter part of the 20th century. Individuals and groups of people made their contributions to a story that everyone shares... one planet, one people; a single theme that brings together all the words sung through various voices.

To illustrate this point, listen to the following as if they were on a single album. "Listen to the Music" (DOOBIE BROTHERS) and take a "Journey to the Center of the Mind" (AMBOY DUKES). Within "StarRider" (FOREIGNER), "Stargazer" (RAINBOW), and "Starship Trooper" (YES), the "Mission" (ELECTRIC LIGHT ORCHESTRA) of the "New World Man" (RUSH) is clarified. In order for you to easily "Roll With the Changes" (REO SPEEDWAGON), remember that it is "Your Move" (YES), so "Let the Day Begin" (CALL). In the light of a dawning Age we can trace the theme linking these (and other) songs together in the telepathic "Silent Lucidity" (QUEENSRYCHE) of the upper dimension. We hear and see the reality of a New Oz.

There are a great many instances to be found when applying this concept of a New

Oz to popular music in general. In addition, there are many other examples that are not quite so obvious. Parallels in pop music also deal with the symbols of civilizations that were created by the survivors of the Atlantis cataclysm... Atlanteans that escaped to other land areas on planet Earth: the Egyptians; the Mayans; the Incans; the Druids... and the Americans. Some of this material even deals with the story of Atlantis on a *planetary* scale.

Look at the details of what have become the two most popular "best-selling debut albums" in Rock music history. During the decade of the 1960s, the most prolific songwriting team of that era introduced their first album *Meet the Beatles*. With John (lead guitar), Paul (inverted bass), George (rhythm guitar), and Ringo (drums), the BEATLES quickly became a world-wide sensation. The group went through the "Paul is dead" episode. At the end of the decade, the BEATLES expired. Paul wasn't dead, however, for he came back in the 1970s with WINGS. You should realize that this "Paul is dead" episode is a re-telling of the ancient Egyptian transformation story, where the scarab beetle appears to die, goes through a metamorphosis, then returns to life with wings... transformed into a flying being.

The *Meet the Beatles* album remained at the top of the heap until the year 1976, when another new Rock group appeared on the musical horizon; their debut album sold even more than the BEATLES. This new group was named BOSTON.

Pictured upon the cover of the first BOSTON album is a scene that tells of a time before this solar system even existed; vehicles escaping a dying planet. This is the "secret knowledge" contained within the story of Atlantis. The vehicles are a form of guitar, and they symbolize the thought-transference of interplanetary civilizations through the "vehicle" of music.

Perhaps the one single recording of the 1970s that best sums up the emergence of a New Oz into our world of today is the double album (four sides) *Tales From Topographic*

Oceans by YES. Whereas the BEATLES can be seen as representing the Atlantis survivors through Egyptian symbols of their name, this album by YES represents the Atlantis survivors as symbolized by the Maya civilization. You will find within the lyrics of *Tales From Topographic Oceans* a detailed description of the birth of the New Age.

The cover of this album is also visually enlightening. On this album cover you will find a full moon rising directly behind a Mayan pyramid. In the foreground, a group of fish are swimming away from the pyramid. The *symbols* are better understood when you realize that the Maya were known as the keepers of *cycles* of time. In Mayan picture-writing, the start of a new cycle upon planet Earth is always indicated by the image of a group of fish immediately before the start of a new cycle.

Topographic Oceans was recorded and issued at the very end of 1973... the new cycle (the New Age) centers on the year 1976. If you are still quite unfamiliar with pop music, and all that you can do is look into one Rock band, it would be more than worth your time and effort to investigate the lyrics of YES albums issued in the decade of the 1970s.

Incidentally, there was an insignia used by YES that appeared on their earlier album covers drawn by artist Roger Dean... a sort of logo in the form of an "airship". On these albums, this "vehicle" is always found in some sort of a planetary atmosphere. However, there is another instance of Roger Dean's artwork that was used by another group. By looking inside of the *Magician's Birthday* album by the band named URIAH HEEP, you will discover that this "vehicle" has touched down upon the surface of a planet. This album, the *Magician's Birthday*, was used during the decade of the 1970s in exactly the same *symbolic* way as a 6,000 year old Egyptian heiroglyph... to signal the start of a new cycle of time upon planet Earth.

Survivors of the planetary Atlantis that settled in Egypt were the keepers of cycles of time. In Egyptian picture-writing, the start of each new cycle was symbolized by the arrival (the birth) of *The Magician.* In Egyptian heiroglyphics, the Magician (or Wizard) was the initial picture (card) in a series of related pictures; the "A" card. You can find this *symbolism* in the world today in the first letter of our alphabet. It is also used in music. In a band or orchestra, the pianos are all first manually tuned to the note of "A" (440 cycles per second), and the other band instruments are then tuned to the piano. In the emergence of a New Oz within today's American society, both in the technology and in the 5th dimension, the symbol of *The Magician* is represented during the 20th century as the Wizard of Oz.

Sometimes, just the name of a band is enough of a clue for you to investigate their albums. A popular group that symbolically relates by name to New Oz technology is the ELECTRIC LIGHT ORCHESTRA. Besides the lyrical content of some of their songs, look at the cover of ELO's *Eldorado* album... the picture should be easily recognized. Do you remember ELO's *a New World record* tour during 1977? That was the production in which a giant "flying saucer" landed onstage, then the top of the craft lifted to reveal the band riding inside of the ship. Listen closely to the lyrics of that album, then look at the back cover... you will find "the seven stars" of the ELOhim.

With the foregoing information in mind, you can now go out into the world and perform your own investigation of the story that is superimposed on the history of popular music. There are a great many instances to be found in names, lyrics, and album covers. If you still need a little help, try reading the last two chapters of this book for some clues.

As a final item in the story of Rock music, would you believe that there is a song that was recorded using two different speeds, two separate timeframes? First, find an album by Jimmi Hendrix that has the track *Third Stone From the Sun* recorded on it. Put the album on a variable speed turntable and play this track at its normal speed of 33 1/3 rpm. What you hear now at the normal speed is the song as most people have listened to it. Now play this track again, only this time increase the speed to 78 rpm. At this higher speed (higher rate of vibrations) you will now hear a ship entering this solar system and preparing to visit planet Earth.

You have just demonstrated the "slow motion" aspect of the emergence of a New Oz. While immersed in time on Earth and living a daily life at a "normal tempo", there is so much going on around you that some things are not immediately apparent. They only become visible when all of the "time" has been removed... when you can speed up the flow between things and events so that you can see interactions that span vast distances in time. The New Oz reaches back in time for thousands of years.

> *'Isn't life strange...*
> *A turn of the page*
> *can read like before*
> *could we ask for more?"*
>
> **MOODY BLUES, 1972**
> *Isn't Life Strange*

6: Movies

"Show me, don't tell me."

RUSH, 1989

Show, Don't Tell

In addition to Rock music, the emergence of a New Oz is also "hidden" within the category of moving pictures... more specifically, in so-called science fiction movies, "sci-fi". Just as in popular music, every sci-fi movie does not relate to the new dimension. However, when you see the pattern built into some of the more popular sci-fi movies, you begin to see the big picture. Movies are another form of New Age education, just like pop music, and everyone enjoys a good show.

Let's start our look at popular movies with a black-and-white sci/fi classic from the 1950s titled *The Day the Earth Stood Still*. In this movie classic's storyline, a "flying saucer" lands in Washington, D.C. An interplanetary being emerges from within the spacecraft. In his hand, this being carries a gift for the people of planet Earth, a "universal translator". The military mindset prevalent in Washington at that time had determined that anyone or anything that was not "one of us" had to be monstrous, overly aggressive, and a threat to the very existence of humanity upon this planet. Weapons were positioned and trained on the visitor from space. When this being offered his gift of goodwill to the residents of planet Earth (the universal translator) he was promptly shot and wounded.... a case of "Shoot first, ask questions later".

What a typical earthly reaction! Perhaps in time the human race upon this planet will realize that it will remain confined to this solar system until mankind learns the art of non-involvement. We need a change of perspective. How can man expect to travel to the stars and interact with other civilizations if man is incapable of coexisting with his own species on this planet? Acting on imagined threats is a no-no. The television series *Star Trek* of the late 1960s emphasized this concept in "The Prime Directive".

At the present time, mankind has concentrated on a purely physical view of this planet based upon the "law of the jungle"... the ego of the most physically dominant is imposed upon weaker egos. If the population of Earth expects to force its way out into the universe by purely physical means, it will fail in this show of force.

There are other methods of travel available between stars and galaxies. The proto-type race of Atlanteans was aware of interdimensional projection. The MOODY BLUES hinted at this concept in their song *The Legend of a Mind*. In books published over the past decade, there are found descriptions of "beam ships" from the Pleiades star system that operate the same as the transporters found aboard *Star Trek*'s starship

Enterprise, only on a much larger scale. For a simple explanation, the Pleiades "beam ships" can cross the huge distances between stars and galaxies by polarizing (shifting) the angle of their molecular spin and "rising" into an upper dimension, then mentally projecting their molecular patterns non-materially... transcending both space and time as known on Earth. (A similarity on Earth would be in radio or television transmission and reception.) These "beam ships" are directed in ways which we would describe as being both mental and musical when operated within the earth plane.

They operate inter-dimensionally, and move in and out of both upper and lower dimensions. The upper dimension has the same relationship to Earth as men-in-air do to fish-in-water. Do you think that a fish knows what is going on in the air-breathing dimension that is "over his head"? To the fish, human civilization is just a fantasy.

Upon the American continent, a new civilization was built by other Atlantis survivors who called themselves Maya, or the "children of time". The Maya were quite familiar with and adept at the use of interdimensional projection, and even had a name for it... *Skywalking*. The Maya believed that their ability to become Skywalkers would be lost for hundreds of years, but would eventually return to planet Earth in a future time... at the turn of the 21st Century.

The Egyptians also shared a very similar point of view, for inside the tomb of Tut-ankh-amun, an inscription was found stating that in the future, there would come a time "... when the wisdom of the ancients shall arise and walk the Earth once more". The time that this re-awakening was expected by the Egyptians centered on the year AD 2000... the turn of the 21st century.

The "return of the ancients" theme has been told in a unique way via a popular sci-fi film. During the late 1960s, there was a movie released with a storyline about a group of travelers who return to the Earth after being away for a long period of time, they return to discover that the world they were familiar with had been dramatically changed. The travelers left this planet at a time when human values guided earthly civilizations; they returned in a "future time" when mankind's animal nature dominated the Earth. *The Planet of the Apes* gives a fresh insight into the Maya Skywalkers as they return to our world... the 5th dimension returns to planet Earth, only to find that "the monkeys have taken over". Like when in Oz, be very cautious of any "flying monkeys" that you might encounter.

Some prominent symbology related to the Maya is contained within the movie classic *Star Wars*:

* the name "Skywalker"
* Luke's "home planet" orbiting a binary (dual) star
* the Maya teachers of enlightenment were called "Ah Kinobi"
* in "Star Wars", the teacher was named Obi-wan (Ben) Kenobi
* "The Force"... the universal source of enlightenment, psychic development, and interdimensional travel.

Another movie was released that fits right in to the emerging pattern... *Close Encounters of the Third Kind*. In this film, beings not indiginous to planet Earth were attempting to make contact with the human inhabitants. They communicated through music (remember the BOSTON album cover). After landing their ship, the beings that exited the craft were all humanoid, for universally we are always recognized as "men"... we are all brothers in spirit and in form, across the universe... no matter what time, place, planet, or star-system.

Finally, there was recently released a movie about beings from the stars that had visited planet Earth in the distant past. Some of these beings had remained upon Earth. They possessed powers of healing and rejuvenation, like the Fountain of Youth. These beings had remained upon Earth in a kind of suspended animation, a transitional stage... "asleep".

These "sleeping" beings were sought by other members of their galactic race when the ships returned to this solar system, and to planet Earth. The present-day Earth-colony of these "sleeping" beings was physically located within the United States, in modern 20th century America. The city in this movie is named St. Petersburg, Florida. The name of the movie is *Cocoon*.

More truth is "hidden" in this story than is at first realized. As the submerged memories of Atlantis resurface within the United States of America, and as the Skywalkers re-awaken within the minds of present-day Americans, the focal point of a New Oz is revealed... a city with the perfect disguise.

> *"... it's been such a LONG time."*
> BOSTON, 1976
> *Long Time*

7: The Focal Point

The perfect disguise. If you want to hide or conceal something from view, an easy way to do it is by *distraction*... by diverting people's attention away from what you are trying to hide. An easy way to trivialize something is to turn it into a joke. Even including the movie *Cocoon*, the present reputation and image of the modern Florida city known as St. Petersburg is trivialized into that of a vacation resort area and residential retirement community; not industrial, not progressive, and not very interesting... in other words, the perfect disguise.

The key that unlocks the doorway into the 5th dimension is the *name* St. Petersberg... "the city of Saint Peter". Saint Peter was symbolized by a key (or keys), and was the person that Jesus called "the Rock" of the Christian church. Saint Peter was also crucified, but in an *inverted* position... upsidedown. In our western culture, Saint Peter is often portrayed as standing by the Heavenly Gate, the *doorway* between this world and the next. How many symbols and metaphors can we find today in this Florida city named for Saint Peter? We have already identified "the Rock" (music).

In October of 1492, Columbus realized his dream... his expedition discovered what was to them a "new world", and in so doing demonstrated that the "flat" world was really round. Twenty-one years later, another Spanish ship set sail for the New World. It was in search of the mythical Fountain of Youth. Juan Ponce de Leon crossed the Atlantic in the year 1513. On Easter Sunday, at the vernal equinox, the expedition of Ponce de Leon discovered a tropical land that he named Florida, "flowery Easter", the land of flowers. However, that expedition only discovered the land; they did not come ashore.

The first exploration of the land area that was to become the United States of America started in Florida 15 years later, in 1528. The Spanish expedition of Panfilo de Narvaez sailed up the western coast of Florida, stopping at a region known today as Tampa Bay. Narvaez came ashore and stood upon a land-mass that the Spanish called *Punta Pinal*, or *Punta Pinales* (a point of pines) almost fifteen years to the day after Ponce de Leon discovered Florida. Narvaez made landfall at *the point* on Good Friday, the vernal equinox, in the year 1528... he was the first explorer of Florida (and America), more than 350 years before "the point" was to became the city of St. Petersburg.

The second Spaniard to explore Florida,

Hernando de Soto, also made landfall in the Tampa Bay area eleven years later, at the vernal equinox in 1539.   Today, his name is commemorated by Fort De Soto Park in Pinellas county, built upon an offshore island at the mouth of Tampa Bay.

In our modern turn of the 21st century world, the city of St. Petersburg is where you will find an actual representation of the Fountain of Youth.   Ponce de Leon was searching for it when he discovered the state of Florida; today a physical Fountain of Youth is located by the Bayfront Center in downtown St. Petersburg.

Also located in this New World city is a monument to Christopher Columbus, which stands at the approach to The Pier, also on the downtown waterfront. The Pier is a five-level structure that resembles an inverted pyramid, and is built off an extension of land that projects out into Tampa Bay. Just like the Great Pyramid, this structure also is used to generate forms in the earth plane.

The physical shape of The Pier, an *inverted* pyramid, symbolizes and focuses the emerging New Age on planet Earth within America, within the state of Florida, and within Pinellas county, "the point". A visual image is inverted at its focal point. The base of the Great Pyramid of Cheops is anchored to the ground (lower dimension); the base of The Pier is anchored to the sky (upper dimension)... remember BEATLE Paul McCartney's "inverted bass". In today's world, The Pier resembles the Temple Beautiful once found in ancient Atlantis... a central pyramid encircled by individual shops from other nations. The Pier was opened to the public during January of 1973.

From November 1975 through the spring of 1979, The Pier was the original home of The Laser... the only city-owned laser sculpture by artist Rockne Krebs, his first "permanent showpiece". The Laser was formally dedicated on the vernal equinox, March 20, 1976. It operated on the water- front sporadically through early 1979, weaving a web of shifting patterns of light throughout the city.

Mechanical difficulties and the cost of replacement bulbs eventually forced the Laser's retirement. In addition to the Fountain of Youth, The Pier, and The Laser, the city of St. Petersburg is also the home of the seventh domed sports stadium in America, the Florida Suncoast Dome... which opened to the public in 1990.

St. Petersburg *should* be known as a city of "firsts": the first exploration of Florida; the first radio station in Florida; the first scheduled passenger airlines (the St. Petersburg-Tampa Airboat Line, 1914); the first city-owned Laser; the first identification system for contact lens that were coded by laser; the first computer controlled planetarium in America (St. Petersburg Jr. College campus on Eagle Lake); the first laser-controlled musical instrument, the "Orchestron"; and the oldest continually operating greyhound racing facility in the nation, Derby Lane.

The Benoist Airboat, a double-winged seaplane, flew twice across Tampa Bay on

New Year's Day, January 1, 1914... the first scheduled passenger airline flights. Jannus Landing in downtown St. Petersburg, where open-air concerts are held, is named for the pilot, Tony Jannus. *Janus* was the Roman god of *doors* and gateways... like St. Peter at the Heavenly Gate. In pop music history, Jim Morrison graduated from St. Petersburg Junior College, then moved to the "City of Angels" and established The DOORS. He now resides permanently in the "City of Light".

In the mythology of ancient Atlantis, both their civilization and technology were powered by a "firestone" crystal, which is quite similar to our present-day lasers.

The very first working model of a laser-controlled musical instrument, the Orchestron, was developed and built in St. Petersburg. The Orchestron was a prototype keyboard instrument capable of reproducing virtually any sound. The first Orchestron was presented to YES in February of 1974, when they performed *Topographic Oceans* in concert at Tampa Stadium.

At the southern tip of the Pinellas peninsula (still known today as "Pinellas Point") the new Sunshine Skyway is found, the longest precast concrete bridge in the Western Hemisphere (a cable supported span that is 15.1 miles in overall length, with a 1200 foot central ship channel). It arches across the waters of Tampa Bay, connecting St. Petersburg and Pinellas county with the mainlands to the south... where the Thomas A. Edison Museum (Ft. Myers) is located.

The main landmark and symbol of present-day St. Petersburg is The Pier... the focal point of the downtown waterfront. From this location, you can see the influences of a New Oz become visible in the world around you. Pieces of the puzzle begin to fit together. Just as in *The Wizard of Oz*, this is an "emerald city" attuned to the color green. The colors of the first high school in the city, St. Petersburg HS, are green and white. The police department outfits its officers in green and white uniforms, and they travel in green and white police cars.

In earlier times, the streets of the downtown section were lined with green benches. This city is the only city to own a green laser sculpture. All county operations are also colored in different shades of green. Similarly, the Mayan *central point* was always green in color, for the Maya told direction by color. A green post was used to mark the center of each Mayan city and town.

Another interesting Mayan tradition was that of the Skywalker. They held the belief that a Mayan (a "Jaguar", the king of the ground) could be changed into a Skywalker (an "Eagle", the king of the sky) by a lightning-bolt transformation process. The transformed Mayan ("Eagle") could then "walk the sky" by entering another dimension of reality. It has been mentioned previously that St. Petersburg is home to the first computer-controlled planetarium in America. This planetarium (mechanical sky walker) is located at Eagle Lake.

The central point of the New Age, when

the Skywalkers were to return, was foretold by the Maya. The following quote is from the Chilam Balam, one of the few authentic Mayan texts that managed to survive the Spanish Inquisition. Chilam Balam translates as "Interpreter Jaguar". To herald the arrival of this expected Maya central point for a new Age, "...from the central region there will be a time when the radiance of the Sun did allow the Eagle to fly into the heavens above a field of lightning bolts." Now that St. Petersburg has been identified as a city that symbolizes this newly emerging and long awaited Mayan central point, let's see how the rest of the prophesy was fulfilled in modern times within the state of Florida.

During the month of July, 1969, in the last days of the sign of Cancer (the Moon), *The Eagle* flew from its launch pad at Cape Canaveral, from the central region of Florida, over Florida weather zone #13 (Central Florida, the "lightning and thunderstorm capitol of America") to carry the first humans to the surface of the Moon. The Mayan prophesy of the Chilam Balam has in our time been fulfilled from within the state of Florida through the technology born in the United States of America.

The *last* Mayan construction on the Yucatan peninsula was at the city of Tical, completed in the year 889, more than 600 years before Ponce de Leon would make his discovery of the state of Florida. We have noticed some amazing parallels between the Mayan civilization, the story of Oz, and the state of Florida that defy all attempts at a logical (scientific) explanation.

The Emerald City and the Land of Oz were created by the American author L. Frank Baum. A similarity between the Emerald City of Oz and the Florida city of St. Petersburg has already been noted... a relationship based on the color green, which also relates to the *central point* of the Maya. Another parallel also exists between Oz and St. Petersburg, and this one is related by *name*.

In the year 1879, Jacob Baum and his new wife Jeannette bought 80 acres of land (at

90 cents per acre) on the Pinellas peninsula and moved there, thus becoming pioneers in the settlement of Pinellas county. In 1888, the Orange Belt Railway tracks ended on Baum's property, at Ninth Street and First Avenue South. The population at that time was just 30 people.

The railroad tracks were extended to Second Street and First Avenue South in 1889. Baum's property and the few stores, post office, and houses around Ninth Street and Central Avenue then became known as "uptown", and the area around Second Street became known as "downtown". L. Frank and Jacob Baum each manifested a form of "upper-lower" relationship in our world.

The city of St. Petersburg was born in the year 1892, four hundred years after Columbus discovered the New World of America. The Maya baktun cycle (400 years) was used to measure major points in time. The next baktun cycle in the United States will be the Mayflower anniversary in 2020.

The first brand *new*, authentic Mayan construction in more than a thousand years can be found today in Gainesville, Florida, on the campus of the University of Florida. Inside of the Florida State Museum, an exact replica of a four-room Maya temple has been painstakingly recreated. This new Maya building has 85 authentic figures, murals, and wallpaintings. It was opened to the public in October, 1977. Additionally, the University of Florida is home of "the Gators" (sounds like "gate"), and the birthplace of "Gatorade", which uses a lightning-bolt as a product *symbol* on its labels.

The Mayan transformation symbol was a lightning bolt. The Mayans who became Skywalkers (Eagles) decorated their clothing and name-glyph with lightning bolts. This is almost identical with the American story about a boy who was changed by a lightning bolt. He was transformed into a person who was able to fly through the air. This transformed being could even visit a place that existed outside of time and space. He wore a large lightning bolt on his clothing; his new name was "Captain

Marvel". How Maya-like! In 1976, the top-rated Saturday morning television show in America was *Captain Marvel.*

Also in the year 1976, the Atlantis Theater opened to the public at Sea World in Orlando, Florida. This theater is found at the edge of a picturesque lagoon, and features a unique "floating stage". Tony Orlando & DAWN were the star performers that appeared onstage at the dedication ceremonies. Tony Orlando & DAWN had the number-one-rated network television show in 1976, "The Rainbow Hour". As you are beginning to see, there are many symbols of the New Oz scattered throughout the state of Florida awaiting your discovery.

By comparing the peninsula of Florida with the peninsula of the Yucatan, an even more amazing link between the Maya and present-day Florida is discovered. To make this visually clear in your mind, rotate the Yucatan peninsula so that it aligns with the state of Florida. With the two peninsulas aligned side-by-side, you will find that seven major cities in Florida are built in almost the same locations as seven ancient Mayan cities, and they represent the very same things in each civilization.

During the decade of the 1990s, the symbol of the lightning bolt can be found throughout Tampa Bay and central Florida, the "lightning and thunderstorm capitol of America". On jackets, hats, and shirts you will find the "lightning bolt" logos of: the Tampa Bay Lightning (National Hockey League); the Tampa Bay Storm (Arena Football League); and the Orlando Thunder (World League of American Football). It seems like magic... the Orlando Magic (National Basketball Association).

The Skywalkers are returning...

*"... and suddenly you hear and see
this magic new dimension."*
QUEENSRYCHE, 1990
Silent Lucidity

YUCATAN PENINSULA

(1) CERROS: a city on a peninsula-on-a-peninsula, point of origin of the Sun Kings.

(2) BECAN and **(3) TICAL:** The area between these two cities was the Mayan gathering place (the Grand Plaza). In addition, the city of Tical was the site of the last Mayan construction.

(4) PALENQUE: a city built around a river, the largest in area of all Mayan cities.

(5) COPAN: the capitol city of the Maya civilization (Home of the Rulers).

(6) TULUM: the "Temple of the Dawn" was built to celebrate daybreak, the first light of day (sunlight).

(7) CHICHEN ITZA: the Mayan exploration of space was primarily from "The Observatory" in this city.

FLORIDA PENINSULA

(1) ST. PETERSBURG: a city on a peninsula-on-a-peninsula, "the (focal) point" of the story of a New Oz.

(2) ORLANDO: the Atlantis Theater, and the Magic Kingdom, the #1 tourist destination in the world.

(3) GAINESVILLE: home of the first new Mayan construction.

(4) JACKSONVILLE: a city built around a river; the largest city in area in the United States of America.

(5) TALLAHASSEE: Florida's government and state capitol are found in this city.

(6) FORT MYERS: home of the Thomas A. Edison Museum (electric light), summer home, and Botanical Gardens.

(7) CAPE CANAVERAL: America's exploration of space is from the John F. Kennedy Space Center.

THE YUCATAN PENINSULA

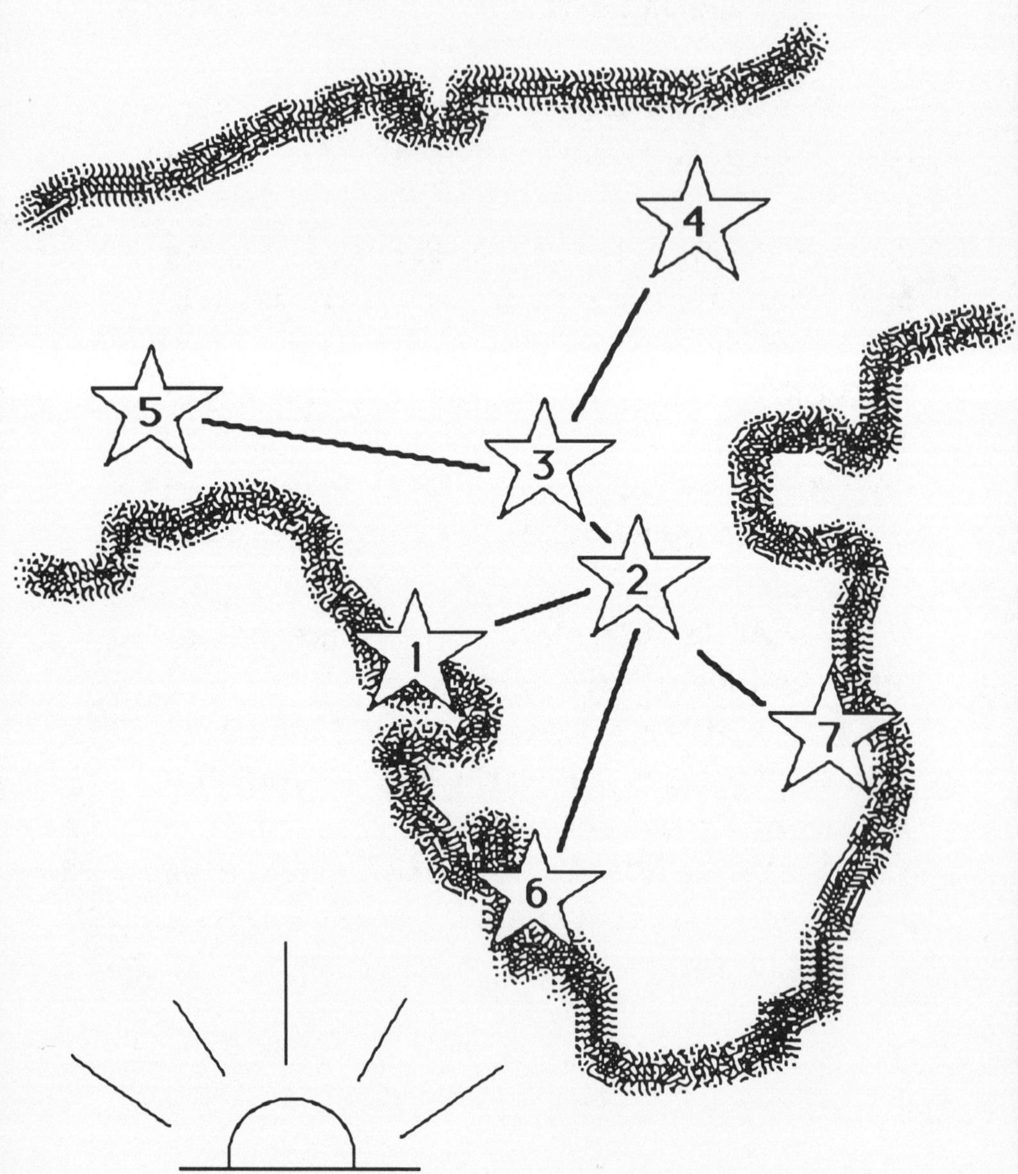

THE FLORIDA PENINSULA

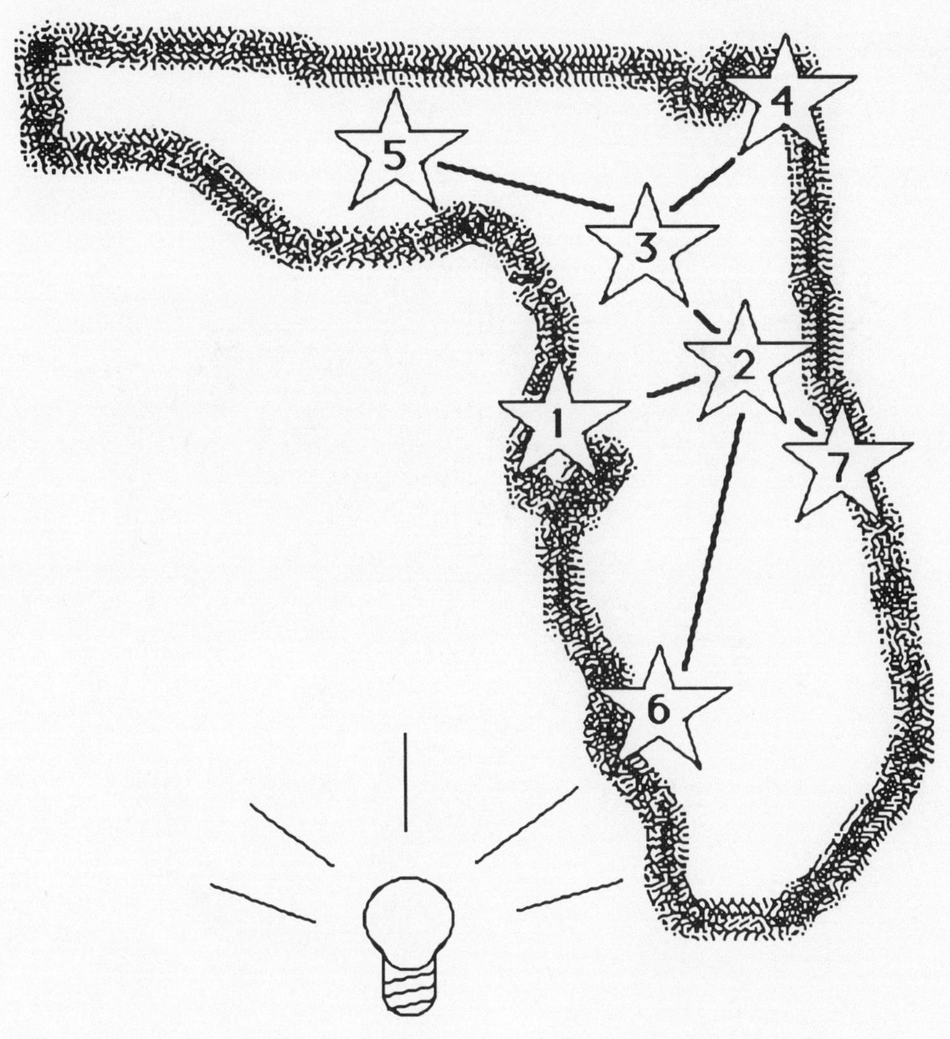

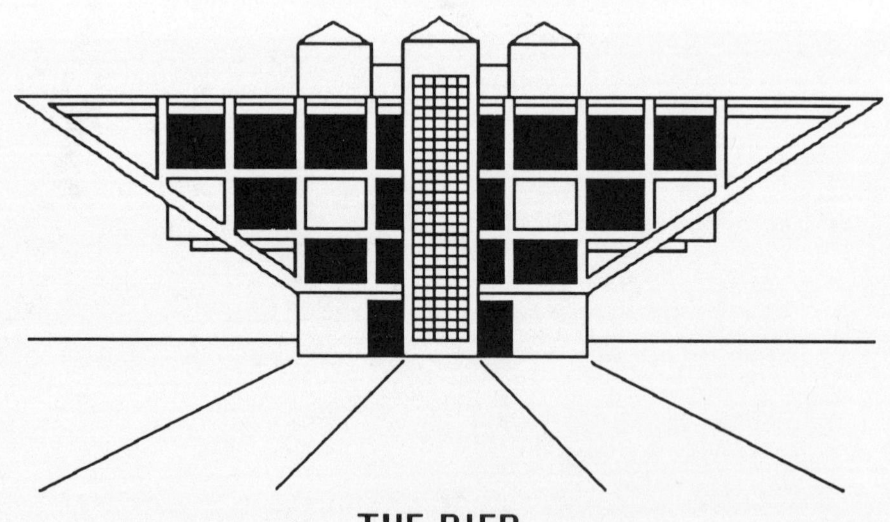

THE PIER
ST. PETERSBURG, FLORIDA

8: The Beginning

> *"Out of a dream, out of the sky,*
> *Into my heart, into my life..."*
>
> **Tom Petty, 1989**
> *A Face in the Crowd*

The ending of an Age is but the beginning of another. It seems that New Oz suddenly appeared out of thin air, but it was phased in gradually. For those who are waiting to cross over into the New Age, the bands, songs, albums, and musical events mentioned in this book should help you to focus on the new reality.

Music and song are generators of human emotional response on the earth plane. Here we can "feel the sound"; in the upper dimension (which is non-material) there is no sound... it is silent and telepathic. Both dimensions are interactive with each other, they are both "reflections" of each other... just like in the Wizard of Oz. The identities in Oz all relate in some way to identities in Kansas. The dream is a shared experience, an inter-dimensional reality... a dream so real.

The emergence of "Rock Music" during the 20th century formed a bridge, a long-lost *doorway* between both dimensions. Once again humanity moves freely from dimension to dimension as we were able to do so long ago. In our own day and time, we are able to pass through a gate that is "new" via a planet that is "old". The emerging Aquarian Age can be focused through the physical shape of The Pier, and so also can the theme superimposed upon pop music. Both of these concepts became visible during the decade of the 1970s. Events emerged and appeared to cluster themselves around 1976, the Bicentennial

Year (a half-baktun cycle). Now that we are able to look back at the decade of the 1970s with all of the "time" removed, the arrival of the New Age can be traced. A pattern emerged as these previously mentioned bands performed their works "live" in the Tampa Bay area.

Album	Band	Date
Demons and Wizards	URIAH HEEP	1972
Magician's Birthday	URIAH HEEP	1972
Close to the Edge	YES	1973
Topographic Oceans	YES	1974
Bicentennial (concert)	EAGLES	1976
Rainbow Rising	RAINBOW	1976
Miracles Out of Nowhere	KANSAS	1977
a New World record	ELO	1977

The names of these groups, the order in which they appeared, and the lyrics in their albums brings the New Oz sharply into focus... a theme that has been a part of our reality for quite some time, but is only now beginning to be recognized. Listen to the music... to the songs and albums mentioned in this book, and especially to the "new" songs of the 1990s. Suddenly you will hear and see a magic new dimension.

By applying the symbols and concepts found within the story of Oz to American history, secrets are revealed... by applying them to our world, a "new ordering of the Ages" becomes visible... a planetary history. The new order is not the same as the old.

*" Oz never did give nothing to
the Tin Man
that he didn't already have."*
AMERICA, 1974
Tin Man

9: PATTERNS

"As I see a new day in me
I can also show it you,
and you may follow..."

YES, 1971
Starship Trooper

Though at first this story might seem to be a "miracle out of nowhere", it is actually a *slow motion* miracle. The paradigm shift to an inter-dimensional reality is now active within humanity, and can be seen in today's world by using the concepts presented in the story of a New Oz.

A "new ordering of the ages" becomes visible in history by using the symbols of Oz, the lyrics found in popular music, and the symbolic reality found within the state of Florida. There are two ways to view the history of planet Earth: (1) you can look for a pattern in all of the names and events of the past that unifies people in the present moment; or (2) you can start with a pattern and look back through time to see the pattern emerge... like the story of a New Oz.

Music was the vehicle transporting inter-dimensional consciousness through humanity and into the earth plane during the later part of the 20th century. A way was prepared for the major reawakening of the 1990s. For those of you who are now inter- dimensionally awake, the message is clear... the dream is not over; it has just begun. We are being given the keys of the kingdom.

The story of a New Oz, the rebirth and development of a civilization within this solar system that originated long ago on a planet long extinct, could not be told until certain things had been built back into this present environment that we call planet Earth. Such is life at the turn of the 21st century. Up until now, it would have been futile to try to explain our true heritage to humanity in terms that mankind could comprehend without the necessary technological development. Try to explain satellite television to Columbus, or how a CD laser functions to Galileo.

Until the time mankind actually began to *experience* the upper dimension "in person", any explanation of it would have been met with disbelief. Out of body experiences are undeniable proof that other planes of life contain their own reality. Most humans believe that the physical is the only reality, they do not perceive that the world of matter is but the garment of our true home... a non-material dimension that transcends time and space. The reality of aliens presently alive on planet Earth is a *fait accompli.*

When will mankind understand that the human race is not exactly what it appears to be? The race of "aliens" from another time and place that were reborn into this solar system are not able to function directly in Earth's three-dimensional plane; they can only experience "time" and life on Earth indirectly, by forming a union of their consciousness with the sentient life-forms that can live upon this plane(t). However, after being born into the material world, these transitory sentient beings (humans) did not remember their origin. The "aliens" could relive and rebuild their memories in this solar system (planetary reincarnation) by developing human bodies as "sense organs" in the lower earthly dimension.

We, the human race, are the "aliens" on this planet. Earth is not the *originator* of intelligent life in the universe; Earth is the *continuation* of life in this time/space. We existed before this present solar system, and we shall survive it. Material reality is manifested through a mind both individual and collective. Symbols and metaphors set the mental pattern of our physical reality on Earth... they did not begin here; they are the memory of our pre-existence. Actually, our true identity is inter-dimensional, half non-material and half physical, coexisting and interacting in each dimension. Mind shapes the material, which confirms the mental.

Throughout the entire scope of Earth's history the theme has been intertwined... we are *both* body and spirit. The story of a New Oz is just a current example told in modern terms without the restrictive "mind control" of some religions. *Think for your self.* You do not have to wait until you die to experience the upper dimension; it is a part of your self. Break on through to the other side. Realize that humans "live out" symbols and metaphors through the events of their lives while on Earth... we follow established patterns, we relive familiar stories, we "re-member" the past, we once again can bring our dreams alive (Oz to Kansas).

Examine all of the different parts of New Oz and see how they fit together mentally... especially music. Awaken your "sleeping" ESP abilities. In order to help you focus, use the symbols and metaphors in the state of Florida example... an "extra sensory peninsula"... where the material reality centered in Florida reveals the mental patterns of a newfound world... a new dimension.

The birth and growth of American technology also provides us with an excellent example. If the start of the 5th dimension in America began in 1976, the birth of technology began 100 years earlier in 1876 with the invention of the telephone. A telephone is a form of electronic voice communication that transmits the human voice (sound). The telephone was invented by Alexander G. Bell (sound). Our three-dimensional physical world is made up of sight and sound, and the birth of technology parallels the birth of a child. Technological sight was born in the year 1879 with the invention of Edison's "electric light". The name Edi-son = eddy currents + sun (sight). After more than 100 failures, Edison succeeded when he coated the filaments of his first "electric light" with element number 76... Osmium (Oz-mium). Edison also invented the first "movie" camera and projector (sight).

One hundred years before technology, a guiding force in the birth of the United States in 1776 was Benjamin Franklin. Ben Franklin experimented with electricity (the kite and the key); he invented the lightning rod, the first electric storage battery, and "bifocal" eyeglasses (two ways to focus). Franklin was the first person to explain how a "tornado" developed.

From the examples given, you can see that the emergence of a New Oz has been spread out over the history of the United States of America. There are other inter-actions in this story for you to find... in relationships between subjects mentioned. For a start, there is an interaction between: (1) the United States, based on 13 colonies; (2) the birth of the United States on July 4, 1776, when the sun was positioned at 13 degrees of the sign of Cancer (the Moon); (3) the Great Pyramid, whose base covers 13 acres of land, the entrance into the pyramid is from the 13th step, and each side is 760 feet in length; (4) the symbols and inscriptions found on a one dollar bill, including a 13 level pyramid; and

(5) the Thomas A. Edison Museum and botanical gardens, covering 13 acres.

The number linking these five items is a *thirteen...* measurement. The Mayan "key numbers" were 7 and 13. The musical scale (6) consists of 13 steps (7 notes), where the first and last are "the same note" an octave apart. The Moon (7) travels across 13 degrees of sky each day, and orbits the Earth 13 times each year. Music and the Moon are the *symbolic* elements of the guiding Elohim. The "spirit of 76" is quite prominent in the emergence of a New Oz... especially 1976.

New Oz is brought to you by a person who in 1972 was nearly hit by lightning, then was lifted up into a dimension *above* time and space. His name just happens to be "Marvel". Get the picture? In silent lucidity, the reawakening Skywalkers ask...

> *"Oh, say, can you see*
> *by the dawn's early light...?"*
> Francis Scott Key, 1814
> *National Anthem*

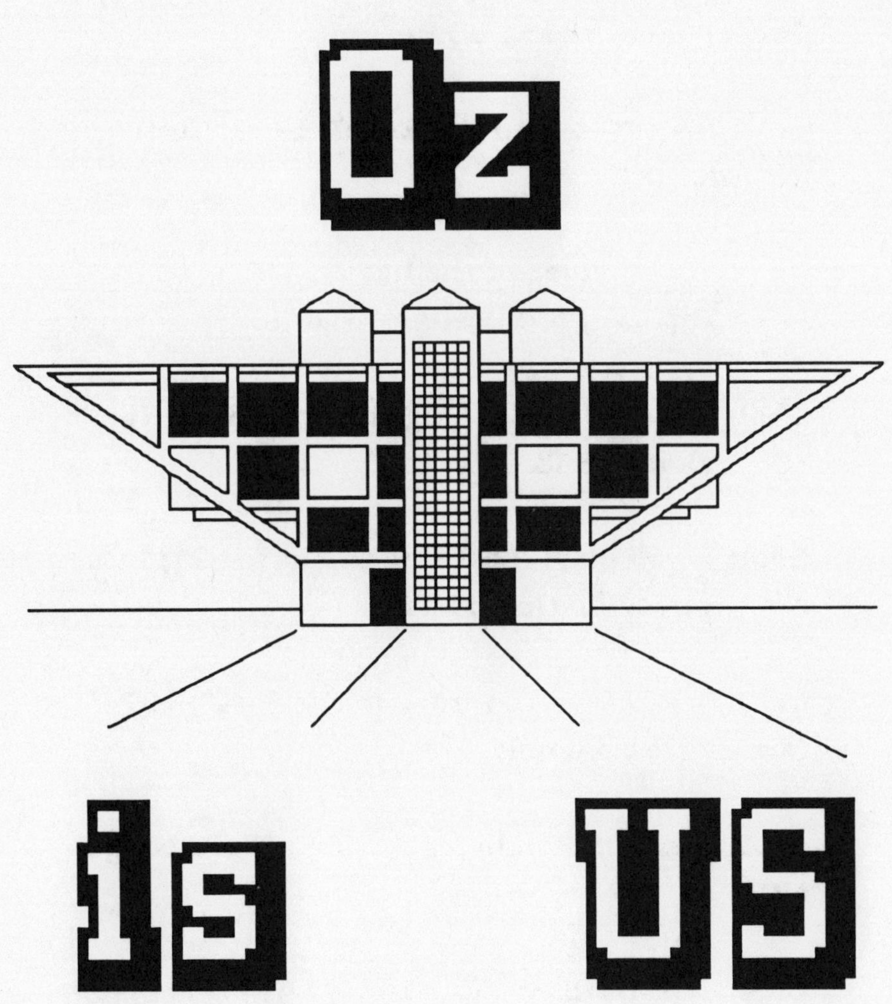
Oz
is US

MUSIC BIBLIOGRAPHY
(artist; song; year; album; record company)

Ch.1: JOURNEY; "Only the Young"; 1983; *Vision Quest* soundtrack; CBS Records

Ch.1: YES; "Close to the Edge"; 1972; *Close to the Edge*; Atlantic

Ch.2: YES; "Dance of the Dawn"; 1973; *Tales From Topographic Oceans*; Atlantic

Ch.2: JESUS JONES; "Right Here, Right Now"; 1990; *Doubt*; SBK

Ch.3: Tom Petty; "Learning to Fly"; 1991; *Into the Great Wide Open*; MCA

Ch.3: CHICAGO; "Saturday in the Park"; 1974; *Chicago V*; Columbia

Ch.4: BOSTON; "Hollyann"; 1986; *Third Stage*; MCA

Ch.4: THE BYRDS; "5D"; 1966; *Fifth Dimension*; Columbia

Ch.5: YES; "Dance of the Dawn"; 1973; *Tales From Topographic Oceans*; Atlantic

Ch.5: MOODY BLUES; "Isn't Life Strange"; 1972; *Seventh Sojourn*; Threshold

Ch.6: RUSH; "Show Don't Tell"; 1989; *Presto*; Atlantic

Ch.6: BOSTON; "Long Time"; 1976; *Boston*; Epic

Ch.7: KANSAS; "Point of Know Return"; 1977; *Point of Know Return*; CBS Associated

Ch.7: QUEENSRYCHE; "Silent Lucidity"; 1990; *Empire*; Capitol-EMI

Ch.8: Tom Petty; "A Face in the Crowd"; 1989; *Full Moon Fever*; MCA

Ch.8: AMERICA; "Tin Man"; 1974; *Holiday*; Warner Brothers

Ch.9: YES; "Starship Trooper"; 1971; *The Yes Album*; Atlantic

MOVIE BIBLIOGRAPHY
(year; movie title; studio; original work; screenplay writer)

1939; "The Wizard of Oz"; Metro-Goldwyn-Mayer; based on *The Wonderful Wizard of Oz* by L. Frank Baum; Noel Langley, Florence Ryerson, and Edgar Allen Woolf

1951; "The Day the Earth Stood Still"; 20th Century Fox; based on a story by Harry Bates; Edmund H. North

1967; "Planet of the Apes"; 20th Century Fox; based on Pierre Boulle's novel *Monkey Planet*; Michael Wilson and Rod Serling

1977; "Star Wars"; 20th Century Fox; based on George Lucas' *Star Wars*; George Lucas

1977; "Close Encounters of the Third Kind"; Columbia Pictures; written and directed by Steven Spielberg

1985; "Cocoon"; 20th Century Fox; based on David Saperstein's *Cocoon*; Tom Benedek

INDEX

St. Petersburg, Florida